BLACK AND WHITE

An Essay on Critical Theory, Freedom, and the Pursuit of Happiness

DOROTHY LOGAN

Copyright 2023 Dorothy A. Logan

print ISBN: 979-8-9875191-1-0
ebook ISBN: 978-1-6678844-9-3

All rights reserved.

TABLE OF CONTENTS

Overview: It is a War of Ideas	1
Part I: Critical (Race) Theory	5
Interlude: Juneteenth	26
Part II: Equality and Equity	30
Conclusion	48
Epilogue	55
References	60
Author's Note	61

OVERVIEW: IT IS A WAR OF IDEAS

When Barack Obama was elected President of the United States, it was as if the entire nation held their breath in hopeful anticipation. Even those who did not vote for him saw an historic opportunity in the moment to heal the racial divide in the country. But instead, it appeared as though things got worse and the divide grew.

When watching the news, engaging Twitter or Reddit (or any other social media platform), paying attention to politics, or even trying to navigate diversity training at work, one might come to believe that racial tensions are at an all-time high. One might even believe that the greatest threat to the fabric of this country truly is systemic racism.

However, this does not always align with the realities people engage or experience in their daily living. Not only do movies and TV shows portray partnerships and friendships and trust between peoples of different cultural and religious backgrounds, but our own IRL partnerships and friendships with actual people reflect the same (or an even greater) level of trust and congeniality – regardless of skin color or culturally divergent childhoods. Most of us have inter-cultural (or interracial, regardless of the meaninglessness of the word) family dynamics based on love, empathy, concern, compassion, joy, and shared experiences.

We cry out in horror when injustice rears its ugly head. We do everything in our power to rectify it, and we see everyone around us trying to help as we grieve with the grieving.

So how can what we are not just hearing, but in many cases *believing*, be so different from what we are experiencing ourselves?

If the "race divide" is as bad as they are insisting it is, if racism is systemic, then how exactly are the solutions being promoted supposed to heal the divide? This is a topic no one dare broach even though it appears as though previous and sometimes similar solutions have served only to divide us further.

It is important to note that racial division is only one form of division in our society today. In an era of identity politics, political polarization, and politicization of every issue and challenge and problem and comment; in an era of assumptions and prejudice where we assign positions and values to people based on a single unrelated characteristic; in an era where social media algorithms are designed to polarize instead of unite; in an era emerging out of masking, home deliveries, remote learning, remote working, online meetings and online events; in an era when we are trying to label ourselves based on what "society" says and how pop culture defines the boxes we are expected to tick; in an era where we are assigning ourselves and others to some vague "group" (and erroneously calling it a "community") instead of seeking meaning and purpose by getting involved in our *actual* local community, we are dehumanizing the humans that make up society and destroying the fabric of our country through isolation and alienation.

With a society made up of alienated individuals, unconnected to any concrete community, it is more likely that the ruling class will be able to manipulate the belief systems of individuals in order to increase their own power.

Americans are no longer exercising the habits that once empowered us. We trust each other less. We cooperate with each other less. We think for ourselves less, if at all. We no longer contemplate, examine, or deliberate over problems because we are not the ones coming up with the solutions. We are detached, and we are okay with that.

The government will take care of my neighbor. The government will take care of me. The experts know best. If something was really important or amazing, we are sure we would hear about it on CNN or Fox or at least on Twitter, Instagram, TikTok, or Reddit.

We are divided. And through that division, we are being manipulated. Americans need to start questioning everything – even our own feelings. Americans need to start thinking critically – and for themselves. Americans must consciously decide how willing they are to simply go along with the narrative pushed by politicians and the media (including social media) instead of writing their own story in a setting and with characters of their own choosing.

Do we want to belong to a group and let that group define us? Or do we want to be a uniquely human individual with deeply personal aspirations and dreams, able to face personal challenges head on and either celebrate our successes or fail forward? Do we want to hand over our thinking and future to those who know better than we do what will make us happy? Or do we want to overcome limited expectations and forge our own destiny?

For the record, I hate the word "race" as it literally has no meaning. It describes absolutely nothing, especially in The United States of America. Society, however, hyper-focuses on this word as a key to ultimate division because there are few concepts and words that evoke as strong emotional responses as anything related to "race." And those who use it (and the word "racism") define it in ways as to inform the narrative that sounds most likely to solidify their position as the morally superior one. It is a word and a concept that evokes visceral reactions because it is such an unnatural one. And in our confusion and altruism and desire to be "good", those who use it and define it for their own purposes use our emotional response to manipulate our behavior and divide us from our fellow man.

Will we let our passions rule us, manipulate us to benefit those same people in power who benefit from the division? Or will principles and an understanding of personal agency push passion and rhetoric aside to reveal true empowerment?

Words have power. But ideas are more powerful yet.

PART I:
CRITICAL (RACE) THEORY

The place most minds go when the topic of Critical Theory comes up is "race" – Critical Race Theory (CRT) – and this is understandable as educators and business trainers are touting its efficacy as a training or teaching tool to address cultural diversity, inclusion, and the like while "conservative" talking heads and influencers are telling everyone how Marxist and therefore very, very bad it is.

But before we can even begin to understand Critical Race Theory, we need to have a working understanding of Critical Theory *in general*. The reason *why* a discussion of Critical Theory in general is important to have has been completely lost in the details and passions of the topic of "race". Not to mention, when trying to figure out *what it is*, those trying to do their own research on Critical Theory are met with contradictions or confusing definitions and then get caught up with whether this is a legal theory, an academic or educational theory, or (from the right) a way to re-write history. It appears that everyone, whether for or against it, wants to talk about where CRT came from, but not exactly *what it is*. And they definitely don't want to discuss why Critical Theory, or where it came from, is relevant.

And it is very difficult to find anything close to a comprehensive discussion on the topic that puts it in full context because Americans like sound bites and simple explanations and hope to avoid saying anything that could be controversial or get them "canceled" or feel pressured to come back with some sort of apology. But to truly understand the relevance to what is going on in our country and politics today, there needs to be a comprehensive discussion about Critical Theory. And when discussing "race" in the American context, this comprehensive discussion is extremely important to have at the outset because without starting there, everyone misses the point.

Such a comprehensive discussion to put the theory in context slips away from the "sexy" headline-grabbing topics and can get boring as the foundation is necessarily laid with the bricks of history and philosophy, held together with the mortar of freedom.

Hegel and Dialectical Reasoning

In his *The Philosophy of History*, Georg Wilhelm Friedrich Hegel introduces his theory of how to interpret history. He rejects the idea that we ended up where we are by meaningless chance. He uses phrases like "the realization of the spirit of freedom" as the rational process through which historical events manifest themselves. He takes specific eras and cultures from the past and applies this philosophy to understanding how these cultures and ideas and ideologies came to be. He further introduces us to a logical reasoning tool called Dialectical Reasoning in order to explain the history-creating process.

Although there are several ways to interpret Hegel, especially through his other more academic works, the easiest explanation of

PART I: CRITICAL (RACE) THEORY

Dialectical Reasoning is that it is a three-part process, that begins with (1) a Thesis. The Thesis is a current understanding or, more simply, the current reality, which is then confronted by (2) an Antithesis. The Antithesis is an emerging understanding, a new idea in response to the current reality, and this confrontation between the Thesis and the Antithesis is then resolved into (3) a Synthesis. The process then begins again with the Synthesis becoming the new (1) Thesis.

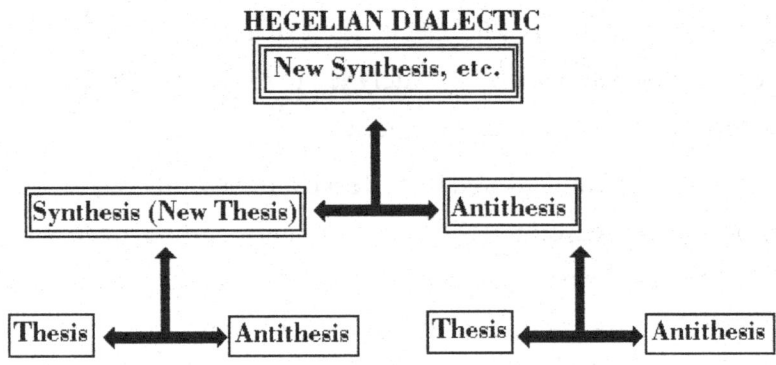

Hegel used this dialectical reasoning as a tool to interpret history. He saw this process as how "progress" throughout history has been made. He examined the past: Ancient Greece and Rome, the emergence of Islam, the rise and fall of the Byzantine Empire, even the French Revolution.

So the reader does not need to read 457 pages of translated German to grasp the theory based on Hegel's own examples, one imperfect and simplistic example might be how The New World was discovered: (1) The Thesis at the time was that the fastest, or only, way to get to India from Europe was to go East. (2) So the Antithesis, the emerging reality or understanding in conflict with the Thesis, was that it might be faster to go *West* to get to India as sailors would not have to go around Africa nor through Asia to get there. (3)

The Synthesis, the new reality created through the resolution of the conflict between Thesis and Antithesis, was the discovery of new continents (and yes, they *could* go west to get there, but there are continents in the way, and *no*, it was not faster.)

A second imperfect and simplistic example might explain how a new nation was created: (1) The Thesis at the time included The Intolerable Acts and taxes imposed on the New World Colonies by Britain after the Seven Years War. (2) The Antithesis or reaction to that reality was The Declaration of Independence and the Revolutionary War, which ultimately led to (3) the Synthesis, a new nation of The United States of America.

Although simplistic and imperfect examples, this is how Hegel used dialectical reasoning: As a way to interpret the past to understand how a people or a culture evolved or developed, and ultimately to explain the process of how humanity got to where we are today.

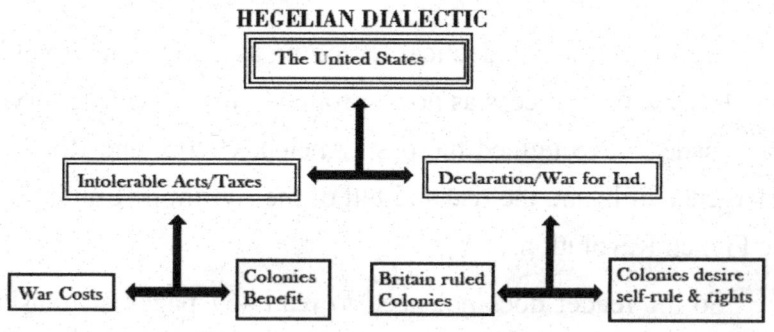

We have a new nation of The United States of America because of the Revolutionary War and Declaration of Independence – and the Revolutionary War and Declaration of Independence challenged the status quo of the Intolerable Acts and British rule of the Colonies.

This logical reasoning tool was never meant to be a way to project the future, but to understand in hindsight how we ended up with the understandings we have today. And although individual passions and desires helped the Spirit of History realize itself, that was, according to Hegel, always unbeknownst at the time to the people themselves.

Marxism

Yes, Critical Theory is Marxist, but conservative influencers seem to believe they can simply say "Critical Theory is Marxist" and everyone will automatically think Critical Theory is bad because Marxism is bad. But *how* is Critical Theory Marxist? And *why* is Marxism bad?

Only after a rudimentary understanding of Dialectical Reasoning can one move to Marx and Engels because they combined their ideas and philosophies regarding Materialism with this new logical reasoning tool of Dialectical Reasoning; but instead of simply using it to interpret history, they used dialectical reasoning to justify their already embraced understanding regarding materialism.

Dialectical Materialism is the theoretical foundation of Marxism. And just for context, Communism is considered the *practice* or implementation of Marxism. Here, however, we are discussing the theoretical foundation of Marxism.

Dialectical Materialism, in very simple understanding, argues that History is a never-ending class struggle or a struggle over (material) resources: The "haves" vs. the "have-nots." So first, Marx applies dialectical reasoning to ensure confirmation of his interpretation of history, but instead of simply using it as an interpretive tool to confirm his own interpretation of history, he goes one step further and uses it as a strategy for the future, a plan to get to a future he desires. And this is the key to the entire argument.

How do I know this? Because he says so. Marx uses Hegel's language, like "universal spirit," but the reader should pay attention to all the words he uses – emphasis added:

> In history up to the present, it is certainly an *empirical fact* that separate individuals have, with the broadening of the activity into world-historical activity, become more and more enslaved under a power alien to them (a pressure which they have conceived of as a dirty trick on the part of the so-called universal spirit, etc.), a power which has become more and more enormous and, in *the last instance*, turns out to be the world market. But it is *just as empirically established* that, by the overthrow of the existing state of society by the communist revolution and the abolition of private property which is identical with it, this power, which so baffles the German theoreticians, will be dissolved; and that then the liberation of each single individual will be accomplished in the measure in which history becomes transformed into world history. (Marx, 1845)

Go back and read that three more times because in addition to the "will-bes", there is a lot packed in there.

Marx sees history as a struggle for Liberty from an enormous power.

According to Marx, "this time" that enormous power is the market, but this enormous power could also be God, the social constructs of an ethical conscience, or… "the system." In Marx's case, he is arguing the enormous power people need to be free from is "the market."

Marx's Thesis is that the market makes some people wealthy at the expense of the others. The capitalists are in control of all the wealth, and therefore he sees them as being in control of the market. But then he argues it was the laborers who accumulated that wealth for the capitalists, and the capitalists are the ones who are just keeping everyone else down, oppressed.

And here is where the dialectic becomes strategy for the future instead of interpreting the past. (1) Marx's Thesis is that the Market enslaves the masses. (2) And his Antithesis reflects what is necessary to pursue a strategy, *not* to interpret how we got to the enslavement of the people by the Market. (2) The emerging idea is that the masses *should be* liberated from the enormous power of the Market. Marx's plan, his Anti-thesis movement is to abolish the market, abolish private property, and overthrow the capitalists. Because then (3) the evil capitalists cannot gain from the labor of others and instead fall under the economic hand of the masses, in other words, Communism (his Synthesis).

This is not an interpretive dialectic as envisioned by Hegel to understand the evolution of history. This is a strategy. A strategic dialectic. One which we have seen *does not work*. Individuals do not need to be liberated from the market. The Market is, by definition, free. It is not under the control of anyone, not even the Capitalists. One just needs to understand how to engage the market. And, in fact, because the market is free, we live by market principles in every area of our lives, not just in economics. This is a huge problem for Marxism.

However, once the market is abolished, someone or some entity indeed needs to make sure the functions of the market (the information the market provides, the goods the market provides) remain in place, someone like a group of central planners. Thus, the money and power once again find their way into the hands of the few who are trying to control market functions at the expense of everyone else.

This is why Communism does not work. It replaces free choice and private property with dictates, plans and force. Utopian socialism cannot work if there is *any* corruption on the part of the central planners, and power corrupts.

Strategic Semantics

But did you also notice how Marx uses statements of fact and even emphasizes these "facts" that are *not true*? It is a very effective rhetorical tool. Just state something as a fact and it is now a premise upon which your logic can be built. The veracity of the fact cannot be questioned because it is confirmed by your theory.

And this is where all the conservatives get it right without explaining why. Black Lives Matter *is* a Marxist organization, but not simply because it was founded by Marxists. Instead, it is Marxist because it was founded under the belief that there is a *struggle for liberty from an enormous power*. Remember, for Marx, the enormous power was "The Market."

The Power Dialectic

Critical Theory is a power dialectic. It builds upon the work of Marx and Engels in that (1) it uses dialectical reasoning to ensure confirmation of a particular interpretation of history; (2) it sees history as a struggle for liberation from an enormous power; and (3) then, in addition to using it as justification for their interpretation of history, it is used as a strategy, a Plan for power reversal.

PART I: CRITICAL (RACE) THEORY

Even though Americans talk about critical race theory (or critical gender theory), the true goal is found in understanding what critical theory itself is, and the goal of critical theory is what makes it relevant (and/or "bad"). The goal of any Critical Theory is *a reversal of the system.*

How it works

In Critical Theory – when designing a strategy for a power reversal, the first thing that must be done is to divide people into two "groups", and they must be exclusive (discrete) groups. No one can belong to both groups. Because in a *power reversal strategy*, the entire goal is to take power away from one group and give it to another. They believe this is the *only way* to liberate the second group from the *enormous power* of the first group.

In Critical Theory, The Thesis (the current reality) is that Group Z is in power.

However, in critical theory, there is no antithesis or emerging understanding juxtaposed to the thesis like Hegel discovered by examining the past. No, instead of an antithesis, there is an ANTI-Thesis: The appearance of an idea in direct opposition to the thesis or the negative value of the Thesis.

If the **Thesis = Group Z in power**, the **ANTI-Thesis = an ANTI-Z Movement** – pushed by **Group (- Z)**.

The Synthesis, in Critical Theory is not a resolution of conflict or a new reality that accounts for a previous understanding synthesizing an emerging understanding. Instead, the "Synthesis" of Critical Theory is the *goal* of the Anti-thesis, which is, of course, a reversal of power. The "Synthesis" is the new reality after Group Z is overthrown by Group (-Z).

Synthesis (New Reality) → Group (-Z) is in power.

Now, before examining this through the lens of CRT, let's test the hypothesis using another (slightly less volatile) example. If the foundational hypothesis of Critical Theory as a plan for power reversal remains intact when testing the hypothesis through the lens of Critical Gender Theory, only then does it make sense to test its reliability against CRT.

Critical Gender Theory

I am a feminist. I believe in the intellectual, political, legal, spiritual, and moral equality of women. I fight for the advancement of women, for their recognition when due, for their protection from immoral, unethical, illegal, and unjust treatment. I fight for our differences from men to be honored and even revered. I want women to know how amazing and strong and powerful they truly are, and I want men to know how amazing and strong and powerful their women are.

But where I want to stop female genital mutilation and child brides and sexual slavery, where I want to elevate women's minds over their bodies, their intellectual capabilities over their physical limitations, where I want them to be honored for their differences and held in the same esteem as their male counterparts – or even in *higher* esteem because of the obstacles they had to overcome that their male counterparts did not – other people who call themselves "feminist" want something very different. For them, it is not about sharing power, it is not about equal opportunity or education, it is not about equal dignity nor about equal respect. These other people who call themselves feminist see the world very differently.

For them, their reality, their Thesis, is simply: Male Domination. The reality they ascribe to is that we live in a misogynistic, patriarchal society (read system) where men are oppressing women.

So the ANTI-Thesis seeks to bring about a "Synthesis" that entails a power reversal where the new reality assigns power to the current "out-group," and this Anti-thesis will be the negative value of the Thesis.

If the Thesis is Male Domination, the negative value of the Thesis is ANTI-Male Domination. The negative value is *not* female domination. No, it is domination that is Anti-male.

Critical Gender Theory is not about equality of the sexes, recognizing their differences and honoring them. It's not about elevating accomplishments of women in a traditionally male dominated society. It is not about protecting women from predators or unjust or illegal acts or from undeserved retribution, nor is it about providing women political and legal equality within cultures where they are currently seen and used as chattel. It is not even about taking the focus off a woman's appearance and putting it onto what she can contribute or does contribute to society. No.

It is about wielding power that is Anti-male.

Think carefully. Why is transgenderism so important to the cause? Why is homosexuality so important to the cause? Some argue that the end goal is to eliminate differences between the two genders, but that is *not* the end goal. The transgenderism movement (birthed out of the successes of the homosexuality revolution) seeks instead to *eliminate men* – at least as a concept. The movement attempts to demonstrate that men are completely and utterly unnecessary. Women can be better men than men ever were. And men, well, they can be turned into women.

The synthesis, the goal, is to eradicate all maleness. This is also evident in the argument now being made that *all* masculinity is toxic masculinity. The Anti-thesis is a push against maleness. The Synthesis (which is no synthesis at all, just the strategy's goal) is a power reversal that minimizes the role of men to the point of elimination.

As a woman, I *almost* understand this goal. I once said I hated men – all men. But I was lumping the good in with the bad. The difference is, in Critical Gender Theory, there are *no good men*. Proponents of the theory take the attributes of their rapists, abusers and oppressors, of all the jerks they've ever met, and characterize *all* men this way. Haven't you heard it said, "All men are rapists"? "All men are misogynists"?

But for me, eventually, after some personal and professional growth, and some healing from my own personal trauma, I realized I did *not* hate men. I LOVE men. And how they are *different* from me. I *love* my father. I *love* my husband. I *love* my son. And when we look at the attributes and character of individuals, we can judge the individual based on themselves, *their* attractiveness, *their* intelligence, *their* cruelty or kindness. The way *the individual* behaves or thinks.

Generally, we don't judge the ones we love based on the actions or behaviors or thoughts or appearance of someone else or some group they belong to, nor do we assign the good attributes of the men we love to the entire world of men as a whole. There are good men whom we love, and yes, bad men whom we would rather see in prison or dead.

But the *power* dialectic is always a *group* dialectic. One group must always be the oppressed, and the other group is the oppressor.

This group dialectic does not recognize individuals. This is why proponents of Critical Theory will not say there can be "good" and "bad" people in every group. They can't. It undermines their strategy. It negates their philosophy.

Critical Race Theory

Critical Race Theory, frankly, is actually the best lens through which to understand the actual goal of critical theory in general and further confirms the foundational hypothesis that it is about power reversal.

What is the *stated thesis* of the Group Power Dialectic of Critical Race Theory?

Answer: White Supremacy/systemic racism. These ideas are coupled together. And this is very important. The system is White. The system is Racist. Racism is bad. So everything in the existing dominant culture, read "system," is White; everything White is Racist; and thus there is systemic racism. That is their Thesis.

Everything in society is "White". Societal norms are White People norms. It is not about the color of one's skin either. If you think the constitution is a good governing document, you are White. If you think work ethic or experience or reliability should factor into salary or job offer or exam score, you are White. Traditional marriage is a White value. If you believe in individual liberty, individual responsibility, individual thought, you are White. And everything White is *automatically bad*.

This is why Tim Scott is called White and why Larry Elder can be a White Supremacist. This is why they don't care about Black police officers. Policing is White. The entire system is White. Policing is part of the system. And just like the market had to be abolished according to Marx, according to Critical Race Theory, the *entire* White system must be torn down.

This is why it is okay to burn black businesses to the ground, steal from black-owned companies, and disregard the law; because those businesses, even though the color of the owner's skin is not "white," they bought into the White System. Therefore, they are part of the system that needs to be abolished.

The goal of CRT then, is to bring down the entire existing system. But that is the goal of critical theory in general, which is why Critical Race Theory is the best model through which to demonstrate the strategy of the power dialectic. CRT proponents actually admit tearing down the existing system as their goal.

Critical Race Theory is not about equality nor is it about diversity or inclusion into the American dream. It is not about equal opportunity. It is not about individual rights. It is not about due process. It is not about individual success or even quality of life. It is about bringing the entire system down.

The challenge for the reader now is to start thinking about groups that may not have made sense before in this new light of Thesis, Anti-thesis, and "Synthesis" (as the goal). The two labels that have received the most attention in recent years are Anti-fa and that of "anti-racism."

Anti-fa is not anti-fascist as in "against fascism." It is a fascist ANTI-Thesis to combat the Thesis of individual liberty. Fascism is the negative value of individual liberty.

Likewise, Anti-Racist is not "against racism." It is a racist ANTI-Thesis to combat the Thesis of Color Blindness and Equality and Equal Opportunity. Racism is the negative value of the equality of all men, the negative value of color blindness, the negative value of equal opportunity.

The idea of equality of opportunity, remember, is part of the System. And it is a White system. The only way to combat a White system is to destroy the notions therein, like individual liberty, individual responsibility, equality, natural rights, work ethic, marriage, and education.

This also helps make sense of why *criminals are their heroes*. Criminals are Anti-System. The police tell you to stop, you go. Police ask for your name, you refuse. The White system wants law and order? They desire lawlessness and chaos – the negative value.

I remember wondering in 2014: "Michael Brown? Really? That's the best you can find for your heroes?" They ignored Corey Jones (2015), which was an excellent example of a tragic event that could have produced positive change in policing if addressed correctly. Do you remember the name Botham Jean (2018)? Probably not, but that was the case where the female officer went into the wrong apartment and killed its resident: Another missed opportunity to produce meaningful change in policing policy and practice. Corey Jones and Botham Jean and even Elijah McClain (2019), an unarmed man whom the police shot unprovoked…these victims *could not be the heroes* of the cause. Because they *were not criminals*.

Corey Jones was a good guy. He played drums for his church band. Botham Jean was an African immigrant whose family forgave the officer. Although situations where highlighting necessary policy changes could have led to better policing, the victims were not the profile of a hero for the cause. The cause, the goal, is not to implement better policing practices. The cause, the goal, is the tearing down of the system.

Thus the heroes have to be Criminals. *Must* be Criminals. And this is why the George Floyd case (2020) was perfect. The hero was a criminal. And everyone was on board with the police officer being in the wrong – because he was. The scenario was perfect for the cause.

This is one of the things that started making sense to me in 2020. For the longest time I could not figure out why all the heroes in the BLM movement and the abolish-the-police movement were criminals. It's not because all victims of police brutality and misconduct are criminals. It is because only criminals can play the role of the ANTI-Thesis, being as they are *inherently* ANTI-System.

And this is also why to those in the movement, *all* police officers are bad. Remember, someone can belong to only one group, and this is why those embracing the movement cannot admit there are some bad police officers *and* some good police officers. In a group power dialectic seeking a power reversal, one can either be a member of the bad System group or belong to the *good* group fighting the System. Police are part of the System. Therefore, they are all bad.

What about "Dear White People"? This idea of white fragility, white guilt, and that to be "woke" is positive and morally superior? If someone buys into any of that, it means they are on the ANTI-System side. They are "allies" with the movement. It is understood that "woke" White people agree that the existing system and its values – all of it – needs to be destroyed.

Unfortunately, the people who see "being woke" as advancement, as a step toward equity, and feel virtuous for embracing it and defending it, have given the Anti-System, or Anti-Racists, the battle wins they need to believe ultimate success is possible. And they have indeed empowered the Anti-System movements to advance their agenda. They are making inroads in corporate training and education. They are wearing society down.

And all they have to do if you disagree with them is call you "racist" because they know that is the worst accusation out there – because *we all hate racists* – which, by the way, fairly indicates we are not racist and obliterates the notion that there is systemic racism. If only everyone would realize this particular accusation actually negates the movement's own theory, it would stop the movement in its tracks. But as Thomas Sowell says, "Some things are believed because they are demonstrably true, but many other things are believed because they have been asserted repeatedly and repetition has been accepted as a substitute for evidence."

And we now have an entire generation, a nation of students and young people exposed to this narrative, buying into the false "facts" that the movement set up as their premise to prove their false facts to justify their strategy, and then the entire strategy is further being justified when the false facts and premises are being held up as the moral standard by celebrities, influencers, politicians and the media.

Logistical Problem for CT Proponents

When they come out and say out loud what their goal is: to burn the entire system down, to eliminate everything that made this country great, starting with natural rights, natural equality and then individual liberties and individual responsibility, people start to see the absurdity.

The cry was, at first, "Abolish the police!" The initial gut reaction was, "Wait. What?! They want *more* crime?" Yes, yes they do, actually. Remember the goal! But when people started questioning this war cry, the movement seemed to recognize how absurd it seemed to the masses, so they start back pedaling to: "Defund the police."

Yet this seems just as illogical as the first war cry because if there are problems within police departments, those departments need *more* funding for better training and to attract better people. So when even that mantra seemed too absurd, they eventually denied they ever called for abolishing *or* defunding the police!

And therein lies the logistical problem for the proponents of Critical Theory. If the Thesis sees the Anti-Thesis winning, and in this case in 2020, "woke" politicians in blue cities and states caving to the demands of these anti-RACISTS and anti-FASCISTS. If the Thesis sees the Anti-Thesis winning, those who recognize the attempt to abolish the system can combat the attempts, like by giving out bonuses to police officers. Like the anti-rioting, anti-looting legislation and pro-self-defense legislation Governor DeSantis put forward in Florida with officials like Sheriff Grady Judd in Polk County, Florida, ready and willing to take a stand and pledge to enforce such things.

Another Problem for Critical Theory

American culture (the current "system" they are trying to overthrow) is based on freedom and liberty, and these things work. And, unfortunately for the proponents of overthrowing the system, Freedom and Liberty are held together by individualism: Individual responsibility, individual rights, and equality for *all*, with a long-held understanding that "equality" means equality of opportunity for every individual, not equal outcomes or parity between groups.

And while the Anti-System movement tries to combat some of this by reframing history, tearing down statues, redefining words, and introducing concepts like equity, the fabric of the nation they want to destroy works to protect itself. Thus, the real problem for this Anti-System movement is that the very people they need to take power from to eliminate liberty are the free thinkers, the critical thinkers, the liberty minded—and these people will always resist. And they will always *exist*, at least while we have freedom of speech and a place to be heard. Those from whom the movement needs to take liberty will not simply roll over and accept the elimination of their freedom.

The problem for the movement is the people the Anti-System movement needs to take power from are those from whom it will be impossible to take it.

Yet Another Problem for Critical Theory

The movement depends on an "oppressed" or powerless "class of people." (For Critical Race theory, that is supposed to be Black people. For Critical Gender Theory, that is supposed to be Women.) In addition to this, the "oppressed class" must also be able to *clearly identify* the "oppressor class." Blacks are supposed to identify Whites as their oppressor. Women are supposed to identify Men (or at least toxic masculinity) as their oppressor.

But these oppressor groups are not so easy to pigeonhole, so that is where a discussion of intersectionality takes center stage. That path, however, leads to so much cognitive dissonance and hypocrisy that they dare not guide very much foot traffic in that direction for very long.

Understanding the power dialectic, who or what is supposed to be the oppressor class for the entire system Critical Theory in general wishes to abolish? Remember, they argue The U.S. Constitution serves as justification for the oppression, the republic is oppressive, and thus the foundational principles of the system are oppressive.

The problem? *This oppression does not exist.* I am not saying racism does not exist. I am not saying that misogyny does not exist. I am not saying there is no patriarchy or discrimination within the system. I *am* saying, however, that the system in place *does not reward* these attitudes with power. In fact, it does the very opposite.

Being a racist does not get someone a job. It gets someone fired. Being Black does not keep anyone from enrolling in an institution of higher learning. In fact, prospective students will lie about their race (saying they are African American or Native American, for example) to bolster their chances at acceptance into the school of their choice.

And even though they are trying very hard to change this perception, the system they are trying to eliminate rewards and punishes *individuals*, not groups, the foundation of their theory, and there are so many immigrants and people born into less-than-ideal situations who understand that if they don't like their current situation, this country gives anyone the freedom to *change their situation.*

The current reality that they want to eliminate also relies on an understanding of equality of opportunity to the point where if that equality of opportunity does not avail itself, pretty much everyone cries foul and is ready to support the person discriminated against.

Thus, the Anti-System movement must expend an exorbitant amount of time, money and energy to *continually create the oppressed class.* They must constantly work to convince people they are victims and oppressed. And they supplement this effort by trying to convince everyone else that they truly are the oppressors.

Continually. Constantly. They must remind people of their victimhood or oppressed state over and over and over and over because if anyone in that group took a minute to look around, they would see that reality contradicts the narrative. If they started thinking for themselves and started believing they can change their circumstances, that they have personal agency, then they would understand it is only their passive belief system that is oppressing them.

Remember, just like Marxism, Critical Theory is a *false* dialectic. We have to understand that not only does it rely on false premises (lies held forth as fundamental truths), but on group think and identity politics.

INTERLUDE: JUNETEENTH

Just signed into law in 2021, this new federal holiday celebrates the end of slavery in The United States.

As slavery is a part of U.S. history that Americans are and should be ashamed of, I believe it is proper and right to celebrate the end of the practice in this country. This is something the *entire country* should be proud of. It was the first step taken by the man-made U.S. government toward recognizing the actual natural law principles upon which the country was founded. It is baffling, however, that it took more than 150 years for the country to officially celebrate something so celebration worthy.

You may have heard arguments that this is a second "Independence Day" – but only for Black Americans (how short-sighted!).

You may have heard it argued that it is an illegitimate holiday because it came out of the BLM movement in response to the George Floyd incident. (Who cares?)

You may have heard that it is the wrong date (or an inappropriate one) for such a celebration. Maybe September 22 would be a better day, the day President Lincoln issued the Emancipation

Proclamation – or maybe December 6, the day slavery was officially abolished by the Thirteenth Amendment.

Once again, I think everyone is missing something profound with all arguments for and against this holiday. So, first a quick history lesson from history.com because without it, the holiday does not may any sense!

The Emancipation Proclamation *was* issued by President Abraham Lincoln on September 22, 1862, which declared "as of January 1, 1863, all enslaved people in the states currently engaged in rebellion against the Union 'shall be then, thenceforward, and forever free.'" (Nix, 2015) And The Emancipation Proclamation basically "freed" slaves in the Confederate states.

However, "In Texas, slavery had continued as the state experienced no large-scale fighting or significant presence of Union troops." (Nix, 2015)

So while the Union troops marched through the South, news of emancipation (liberation – freedom) was taken through the Confederate states, and after hearing the news, freedmen fled to the North under the protection of the Union troops, and all still during the war. But because no troops ever really made it to Texas until almost three years later, it took pretty much until the end of the war for the good news to reach those enslaved in Texas.

June Nineteenth (Juneteenth) "marks the day federal troops arrived in Galveston, Texas in 1865 to take control of the state and ensure that all enslaved people be freed." (Nix, 2015)

But here is where it gets interesting and relevant: Even then, even after the troops arrived bearing the good news and to ensure emancipation, *some* enslavers in Texas withheld this information from the freedmen until the harvest was brought in that fall. And this is the key to the profound lesson everyone seems to be missing.

A year after the good news was brought by Union troops, "freedmen in Texas organized the first of what became the annual celebration of 'Jubilee Day' on June 19." And this is a holiday that has been celebrated in some circles in Texas ever since, but not truly recognized anywhere else in the country (before 2020 or 2021), not even by descendants of slaves from other states in the South. (Nix, 2015)

So, would September 22 be a better day to celebrate Emancipation? Should December 6 be the official holiday to celebrate the fact our government was finally falling in line with its foundational principles and taking responsibility for its past failure to do so? Or should we be celebrating the end of slavery on January 1, when the Emancipation Proclamation was supposed to go into effect? That is now a moot point. We have chosen June 19. And in my mind, I believe the date is *preeminently appropriate*. Why?

First, it demonstrates that someone can be free without knowing they are free. The slaves in Texas were legally freed, but they never knew it. It demonstrates that the freedom of a group of people can be recognized by some but not by others, and maybe not even *by those who have been freed*. And second, it reminds us that there will be those who intentionally lie, telling people who have no reason to believe otherwise that they are *not* free (like the enslavers who wanted to keep the knowledge from the people who would be bringing in the harvest that year), even though natural law and our founding documents declare otherwise and even though codified in our governing document, the U.S. Constitution.

Knowing this history is also *preeminently important*. It points us back to the Declaration principles found in the Preamble that it is *self-evident* (no one should have to point this out…it is *obvious*) that all men are created EQUAL and are endowed by *their Creator* (not the government, not society, not the school system, not the written law) with certain *inalienable* (undeniable, innate, cannot be taken away) RIGHTS, that among these are Life, *liberty* (FREEDOM), and the pursuit of Happiness (everyone has the right to try to go after whatever they believe will make them happy).

Juneteenth should be a reminder to all of us not to fall for the enslavers' lies. Lies that tell you that you are not free. To be free, we must live as though we are free. Because we are. And we are blessed to live in a country where the government put its recognition of this fact down on paper. We are blessed that we were a nation who took this *obvious* natural law and codified it into man-made, legally and politically recognized law, and yes, that fact should be *celebrated* by ALL Americans as a national federal holiday.

PART II: EQUALITY AND EQUITY

(not to mention Diversity and Inclusion)

This is a famous picture trying to explain the difference between Equity and Equality.

There are loads of similar images. They are of people trying to look over a fence or trying to reach something above their heads (a bell, fruit on a tree, etc.).

And this is the problem. This image does not represent equality OR equity.

And so we must start with definitions. Again. Words matter.

This image implies that Equality is providing resources equally across the board. But it does more than that. Both the equality and equity images imply that all the people want the same thing and are there for the same reason. This is how the argument and the words are being framed: "I want to see what you can see naturally. I need a stepping stool, let's give me a stepping stool." The argument against equality is that if you give resources equally, the one person who did not need the stepping stool still gets one and the person who could use both boxes was only given one box and still cannot see. The argument implied in the image is that equality helps some people but distributes resources unfairly and does not help everyone. It also completely ignores the idea that the tallest person on the left could easily and freely choose for himself to help out those to his right.

This image further implies both that (1) resources are limited and (2) that the entity distributing the resources has perfect knowledge of the needs of every individual and can thus more fairly distribute the resources when we take equality *off the table*.

And I am not making this up.

Directly from the website of the Anne E. Casey Foundation:

The following are definitions of core concepts that can help groups develop a shared language for racial equity and inclusion:

DEFINITIONS AND CORE CONCEPTS

EQUITY

Equity is defined as "the state, quality or ideal of being just, impartial and fair." The concept of equity is synonymous with fairness and justice. It is helpful to think of equity as not simply a desired state of affairs or a lofty value. To achieve and sustain equity, it needs to be thought of as a structural and systemic concept.

EQUITY VS. EQUALITY

Equity involves trying to understand and give people what they need to enjoy full, healthy lives. Equality, in contrast, aims to ensure that everyone gets the same things in order to enjoy full, healthy lives. Like equity, equality aims to promote fairness and justice, but it can only work if everyone starts from the same place and needs the same things.

Let me highlight a few phrases found in these definitions and core concepts.

Equity involves trying to understand and **give people what they need to enjoy full, healthy lives.** Equality, in contrast, aims to ensure that **everyone gets the same things in order to enjoy full, healthy** lives. Like equity, equality aims to promote fairness and justice, but it **can only work if everyone starts from the same place and needs the same things**.

This is a misunderstanding of equality. And that is why definitions matter.

Now the first sentence above seems good: "trying to understand [people]". We should all try to understand others, but equity is first and foremost about outcome: "...and **give people** what they need to enjoy full healthy lives." And they declare that "The concept of equity is synonymous with fairness and justice" and seeks a "desired state of affairs."

You can also see this in the site's definition of Racial Justice.

RACIAL JUSTICE

Racial justice is the systematic fair treatment of people of all races that results in equitable opportunities and outcomes for everyone. All people are able to achieve their full potential in life, regardless of race, ethnicity or the community in which they live.

Again, let me highlight some phrases so you don't miss them. Racial justice is the systematic fair treatment of people of all races that **results** in *equitable opportunities and outcomes* for **everyone**. All people *are able to achieve their full potential in life*, regardless of race, ethnicity or the community in which they live.

Go back and read that again. Equity is about *outcomes*. And did you catch it? All people. *All* people *are able* to achieve their *full* potential in life. When was the last time you met even *one* person you thought was on their way to achieving their *full* potential? I know I'm disappointed with just myself...every day.

But it is worse than that because who is dispensing justice? Who is deciding fairness? Whose definition of "desired state of affairs" is driving the equity movement?

So, not only is the goal impossible, but the only way it *might* be possible is if some all-knowing entity distributing resources *decides for every single person what that person's full potential is*, because "Equity involves [giving] people what they need."

The definition and understanding of equality by the promoters of equity demonstrates that the promoters of equity either do not understand the American concept of equality or are intentionally trying to reframe it.

There are loads of definitions for what people believe American "equality" looks like. From treating each individual the same regardless of each's immutable characteristics to treating everyone, regardless of differences, with the same dignity and respect. And this is where it looks like equality seems to play into the "giving everyone the same thing" argument.

To promoters of equity, though, equality (like equity) is about giving and getting *things*. They are not talking about giving and getting "the same respect" or "the same treatment." They argue that equality, like equity, is about *someone else* determining what *every single person needs* to enjoy full, healthy lives. It is about someone deciding what someone else's happiness should look like. The premise is flawed. Why are we simply assuming, regardless of whether we are discussing equity or equality, that someone else, some *other entity* knows better than we do what will make us happy?

Remember: "Like equity, equality aims to promote fairness and justice, **but it can only work if everyone starts from the same place and needs the same things.**"

Promoters of equity see equality as the wrong way to get to a desired outcome. They argue instead for equity. But to understand every single person, which is impossible, and give people what they *need* to enjoy full, healthy lives necessarily puts "happiness" into the hands of the people doling out what *they* think each person *needs* to enjoy what the all-knowing entity *determines* is a full and healthy life.

What they are describing is the centralized planning of happiness. This doesn't even touch on what *desires* an individual might have – just what some centralized planner believes they *need* to live a vaguely defined full and healthy life. The needs are determined by another entity. Any individual desires are irrelevant to the entity. The standard by which to measure a full and healthy life is determined by another entity. What an individual believes will make them happy is, again, irrelevant.

This is definitely *not* the American notion of equality, nor a proper understanding of freedom or liberty. It is the exact opposite. And so it fits nicely with Critical Theory. The foundational American principles declare each person has the natural right to determine and pursue *their own* happiness. Equity is the negative value of such a notion.

American Equality

Thomas Jefferson wrote in the Declaration of Independence, "We hold these truths to be *self*-evident, that *all* men *are* created equal. (emphasis added)

Really? This is self-evident? Were all men truly created equal? Are we all equal? According to the Anne E. Casey foundation, equality only works if everyone starts from the same place and needs the same things. So were all men (or all people) created equal?

Do we all have the same body type? Do we all have the same intelligence? Do we all have the same abilities? Do we all have the same gifts and talents? Obviously not! Some people are better mechanics. Some people are better doctors. Some people are better vocalists. Some people are taller or stronger or faster or, yes, even better looking! Some people are better at science. Others are better at math or art or music. Others are better test-takers. Some of us have a sense of humor. Others have better hand-eye coordination. We all have different eye color, skin color, hair color. Some of us like to read. Some of us don't. Some of us like to drive, and FAST. Some of us don't. Some of us are men. The rest of us, believe it or not, are women. We are each different from everyone else. We were created unique! With unique individual needs and desires and personalities and styles. So how then could we have been created *equal*?

Besides, not a single one of us started in the same place as someone else. Promoters of equity recognize that, which is how they argue against equality in favor of equity. They argue that some people were born with advantages and this is not fair. So in pursuit of *fairness*, equity appears to desire to *make* those born without advantage "equal" in outcome, with the outcome apparently being a full and healthy life! The equal outcome, facilitated by some outside entity, should be, it appears, happiness for all, when that is impossible.

So what did Jefferson mean when he used the word "equal" and how does that differ from the equity argument?

All men are created equal, but he goes on to say, "and are endowed by their Creator with certain inalienable rights. And…there it is! We are equal in our *rights*! Americans believe in Equal Rights.

Slavery

Even though at the founding of our country there was an entire group of people denied rights by most state governments, and the federal government chose not to defend or protect the rights of those same people, the entire premise of our constitution rests on the inherent rights of *every single person*.

It is important to note that if it is the government that is giving rights, it is the government that can take them away. But if God, or Nature, gives us *inherent* rights, the government violates the inherent, natural law by taking them away. And that was the premise for our War for Independence. That was the premise of the "new" constitution. And, indeed, one of the primary justifications for all the death and destruction the North wrought on the slaveholding South during the U.S. Civil War—as well as the premise for Martin Luther King Jr.'s Civil Rights Movement almost 100 years later.

So even though there was an entire group of people denied rights by the government, those rights did not cease to exist for those people. The rights are inalienable. In fact, it was the entities who *denied* those rights to others who were in violation of the natural law.

Americans believe in equal rights. They must, or the entire government is without foundation.

With the thirteenth, fourteenth, and fifteenth amendments, collectively known as the Civil Rights Amendments, the government finally recognized its violation of natural law. They did this by again codifying the idea that **all** people are entitled to equal protection of the law. And what does the law protect? Our rights! (At least that was the premise at the time.)

So, with the Civil Rights Amendments comes a recognition of – once again – equal rights. They acknowledge the inherent equality of all men. These amendments did not *grant* equality, did not *grant* rights. They *recognized* them. Again. Acknowledging the sins of the nation and reaffirming the original notion of American equality. And promising to do a better job protecting the inherent rights of *all* people.

Equal Opportunity

But Americans' belief in Equal Rights does not end there. It has also led to a belief in equal opportunity. If we have equal protection under the law, if everyone's rights are protected under the law, then everyone has the *same opportunity* to pursue their dreams and achieve their own self-actualization. (As opposed to some all-knowing entity deciding what self-actualization is for you *and* everyone else.)

We have the self-evident, inherent, *equal* right to pursue our own happiness. We do not need to look to someone else, like an all-knowing entity who supposedly knows us better than we know ourselves, to tell us what our happiness should be and what is required to achieve it. No one does. Each individual person has the right to pursue their own unique brand of happiness, to decide for themselves what will make them happy, to stretch the concept of what their own full potential might actually be – as well as the right to fall short of it. (As I do every day.)

Equality is not about giving everyone the same things in order to enjoy full, healthy lives. It is about equally protecting each person's right to pursue their own happiness.

The natural rights listed in the Declaration back this up: Life… Liberty…and…what? The pursuit of happiness. We are free to live our lives as we see fit. We are free to pursue those activities that will make us happy, that which will help us reach that highest level of our own self-actualization.

No one else can determine what our "full potential" is. That is utterly ridiculous.

Nor do we all start in the same place or need the same things. And we definitely don't desire the same things. This concept of "equity" twists the original intent of equality.

If someone is faster and stronger, they might find happiness in athletics, track and field, football, basketball, baseball, boxing, soccer. And if in the course of pursuing this happiness they become the best of the best, they might even have the opportunity to go pro. But just because someone is faster and stronger does not mean they *will* find happiness in pursuing athletics, nor that they necessarily *desire* to pursue a career as a professional athlete.

If someone wants to become a pharmacist, nurse, doctor, teacher, accountant, business owner, they have the opportunity to pursue those goals. The law protects that *opportunity*. It does not and cannot guarantee actual happiness. Many people pursue what they believe will bring them happiness, achieve the goal, and find not happiness, but dissatisfaction.

Americans make a very strong connection between equal rights and this equal opportunity to *pursue* happiness. This is underscored by the fact that when equal opportunities do not avail themselves, Americans tend to cry foul. We recognize the violation! And not just of our own rights, but when the natural rights of others are violated.

Thus, Americans as a group – and again, I'm not saying there aren't any racists or bigots or sexists – but as *society* – Americans base their beliefs about people, whether they recognize it or not, on this idea of Moral Equality. We are inherently equal because we all have the same natural, or God-given, rights. Because of this, Americans subconsciously or even unconsciously make that connection between equal rights and equal opportunity. And thus, this understanding of equality, unlike equity, is *already* a "structural and systemic concept" as part of "the American way." And as part of the American System, this understanding of equality is something CT advocates want to take from us.

So the attack against equality next employs the argument there really is no equal opportunity *because* we all start in different places *and* the outcomes vary wildly from person to person or group to group.

And yes, it is true. Equal opportunity will *necessarily* lead to vastly different outcomes because no one has identical pursuits. We are all different! And we are all complex! And yes, we also all start in different places in life. This is the reality advocates of equity seek to address as one of the evils of society, yet no one can guarantee someone else's happiness. Therefore, no one can guarantee equity. But can't we close the gap?

One way to attack equal opportunity is to shift the argument from equal opportunity to equal *access* to opportunities. In early 2020, I had a student mention in an online discussion thread: "It is evident in our society that not all individuals have equal access to certain opportunities, such as employment or education."

Perception is reality. Equal access to opportunity does not mean we all start in the same place. We don't. We can't. Why single out education and employment? This is true for all areas anyone desires access to. We do, however, each have the equal opportunity to *pursue* our happiness. Thus, we all have equal access to opportunity. The distance between where the door to opportunity opens and the goal, however, can seem greater for some than others. But the door is there for everyone.

Consider "happiness" (whatever that is for anyone because it is different for everyone and that is the point) the destination. For argument's sake, let's call that destination "Miami." Some people start the journey to Miami in West Palm Beach. Some in Atlanta. Some in Tennessee; some in Maine; some in Alaska.

The people who start in West Palm Beach have a shorter distance to go to get to Miami, but the person in Alaska can still start on their way to Miami.[1]

But even those who live in West Palm Beach: How will they get to Miami? Will they take the Turnpike? What if they can't afford

---

[1] "Equity wants to punish people who live closer to Miami simply for being born so close and move people who start farther away closer to Miami. But we all start out at different places with different resources. Equity is impossible, and I will say it again, not even desirable.

it? Will they try anyway and get billed by plate? Go into debt? Will they not pay the bill in time or get held up by a suspended license?

Or they could take I-95. There aren't any tolls. But what if their car can't go over 45 miles per hour? They could take US 1. But what if they don't even own a car? Can they rent a car? What if they cannot afford the gasoline or the insurance? They can ride a bike. Their tires are flat? They don't even have a bike? They can walk. The journey might take longer. It might be more exhausting. It might be much more difficult, and they may not even make it ultimately, but no one is stopping them from making their way to Miami. In other words: The door to opportunity is open. **They are not locked up in a garage somewhere.**

But let's give everyone an automobile, at least! The argument shifts to the idea everyone needs a motorized vehicle to make it to happiness. What's wrong with that idea? Well, even those who start out in cars, their cars can break down. They can get a flat tire. They might run out of gas. Even people who started closer to Miami with more initial resources might decide at that point to give up on their journey, or they could struggle to replace the tire or trade their car for a bike and still make their way toward Miami. People driving to Miami in cars may leak oil that leads to destruction of their engine, or they might end up dead in a car crash, especially if they did not take into account the conditions of the road, the speed limits, or other reckless drivers.

Cautious drivers might be passed by less cautious ones or might find themselves in the midst of a road rage incident.

Some people drive luxury cars. They can't even hear the traffic outside. They can travel faster and in great comfort. In fact, some of them can have others drive them and just "enjoy the ride." But even these drivers and passengers in luxury cars can get pulled over for a ticket or end up in a multi-vehicle pile-up. These people traveling to Miami in luxury could also choose to take someone not blessed with a luxury car with them. But they could also actively and decidedly refuse to help anyone else get there.

Meanwhile, some people are willing to let someone else control their trip to Miami, so they ride the bus. It is slower and might not go *exactly* where they want it to, and they are stuck with people they would never have chosen to go on this journey with. They are all headed toward Miami but with no control over where they will stop along the way, the ultimate destination, or the companions they have in the meantime.[2]

When we tell people they don't have equal access, they believe they cannot get to equal opportunity; and then they believe they cannot get to happiness. When this is not true. There are people with absolutely nothing, not even stable parents, stuck in foster care, who are getting a stellar education. There are those who got a crappy education in grade school but ended up renowned in their fields. There are those who had access to the best education possible and squandered the opportunity.

Think back to your own high school experience. Everyone has the opportunity to go to school in this country. Everyone. In fact, schooling is mandated. Everyone must go. Now, that is a conversation for another day, **but everyone has an opportunity to an education.**

One may argue that not all schools are equal. And they aren't! So, for the sake of argument, let's just say your parents had the

---

[2] The bus ride, however, comes a lot closer to the goal of equity than equality of opportunity as someone else is determining happiness and the route to happiness for those on the bus, and it is a lot less work for the passenger who does not even need to pay attention, and the outcome is more or less the same for everyone on the bus.

financial capability to send you to the best private school in your area. The best of the best. What did *you* do with your educational opportunities? Did *everyone* in your class make the best of the opportunity granted them? Did you? Or did you complain about homework? Did you even do your homework? Did you study for your tests? Did you write and rewrite your papers? Did you do your own research? Did you take every opportunity for community service, extra-curricular activities, clubs, and sports? What did *you* do with your opportunity? Did you live up to your *full* potential?

Even if someone was given access to the best school, there is no reason to believe they would live up to their full potential. Even if everyone had "equal access" to the best education, there is no way to guarantee they would make the most out of the opportunity or even learn the basics. And all these questions could also be asked of those going to the worst school in the worst neighborhood.

Were there others who worked harder? Or maybe others who were just smarter? Were you the top of your class? Or was someone else? Did you give up baseball to join the band? Or give up violin to play soccer?

It is up to us to decide what to pursue. What we think we can be the best at. Then we seize on our right to pursue it. And then, depending on how much ability we have and how much effort we put into the pursuit – that's what's going to determine the outcome. But not even in such a scenario is any given outcome *guaranteed*. There are many events in life that can derail the outcome someone chooses to pursue. (Think illness, freak accident, home invasion, sudden death, bad choices, etc.)

Equal rights and equal opportunities do not guarantee equal results. Even if we could foresee any possible tragedy that might interrupt our journey toward happiness, we are all different! Some of us work harder, put in more effort. Others of us just have more natural ability or a personality better suited for a particular endeavor. And we all pursue something different too. Even if *everyone* had access to the *same* education, the outcomes would be completely different for each person.

Instead of focusing on where people are starting, which equity likes to do, because none of us have equal beginnings, those of us who are familiar with the road should be equipping those with a rough road ahead for the journey. Because the living takes place in the journey. The person starting in Alaska will have to travel through Canada, then across the whole country to even get close enough to see signs directing them to Miami, but what experiences they will have! What sights they will see! What lessons they will learn! What accomplishments they will celebrate! Those starting out in West Palm Beach *miss out on so much*. Those cruising in luxury don't accomplish much or experience much or celebrate much and are comfortable in their complacency.

We should be striving for American equality – the kind that emphasizes equal opportunity. And then rewriting the narrative for individuals within our sphere of influence. Perhaps there is too much individualism in our culture when those familiar with the road fail to inform, encourage, or help those who are in the midst of a difficult journey. But where should the encouragement start? Who should be the primary encourager?

American Equality is not related to equitable outcome or access. It is not about fairness, but directly linked to the foundation of this nation, the bricks and mortar of natural rights and individual liberty.

We shouldn't hand over our responsibility for our happiness to someone else. If we let someone else tell us what our full potential is, if we let someone else set the standard for when we have met that potential or have achieved a full and happy life, we are not free. If we let someone else tell us what a full life means or where our happiness lies, we have exorcised the American spirit of liberty and have instead become North Korea.

But if we treasure liberty and freedom and take responsibility for pursuing our own happiness, we can change our minds, re-prioritize, and decide for ourselves what we need for a full and healthy life. And then use our own gifts, talents, connections, and limited resources to pursue and maybe even achieve our happiness.

Diversity & Inclusion

And as everyone is pursuing a different happiness, instead of the one that someone else told them they should, liberty automatically breeds diversity. Diversity in art and music, diversity in all the arts. Diversity in innovation and business practices. Diversity of ideas. Diversity of skill sets and talents and recreational activities. Diversity of goods and services. Diversity of opinion. Diversity in architecture. Diversity in scientific pursuits. Diversity in style. Diversity in failure – and diversity in success. Diversity in families and friend groups and organizations.

As civil society grows, it eats away at political society, at the tyranny that wants to dictate what is right and good for everyone. As everyone determines their own pursuits, instead of letting someone else (like an all-knowing – impossible! – and all-powerful government) determine their happiness for them, civil society grows. And with the growth of civil society and the shrinking of political society, we see more and more liberty. With more liberty comes more diversity and with more diversity comes more civil society. It is a cycle that can feed itself.

Diversity and Inclusion are always part of the equity v. equality debate, but while liberty produces equal opportunity and diversity, there is no mechanism through which equity and pursuit of *fairness* produces the same diversity of diversity. But promoters of equity do have a good definition for inclusion.

According to the Anne E. Casey Foundation:

INCLUSION
Inclusion is the action or state of including or of being included within a group or structure. More than simply diversity and numerical representation, inclusion involves authentic and empowered participation and a true sense of belonging.

This definition describes the benefits of civil society. And civil society also describes and reinforces true inclusion.

Civil Society

How does civil society do this? What is civil society anyway? (I know there must be a few out there asking this question!)

Civil society is opposed to political society, which consists of all the activities organized on the principle of coercion. In other words, all activities set up by the government as every regulation or law forces Someone Somewhere to do Something. Civil society, in contrast, includes all natural associations, like the family, as well as all voluntary associations like church or synagogue congregations, community clubs, sports teams, private businesses, and charities.

The key word here is "voluntary." Involvement in *civil* society focuses on the voluntary nature of the relationship. Basically, except for your family (which eventually does, in practice, become voluntary), membership or participation in these associations or organizations is completely voluntary. You can choose to go to church or join the community softball league.

These voluntary associations then provide values, meaning, purpose and a sense of belonging to individuals who are participating in them. Think about it: Athletic teams, congregations, and clubs all give meaning, purpose, and a sense of belonging to those who are members of them. And in providing meaning and purpose, these voluntary associations can also be seen as sources of moral authority.

Whereas government, through force of law, seeks to take the lead role of moral authority in the lives of its citizens, civil society provides a moral authority almost as diverse as the people coming together looking for meaning and purpose. And where the moral authority of government has its foundation in its power to dictate what is right and good for *everyone*, what *everyone* needs to be fulfilled, and somehow convinces its people it knows what achieving their full potential looks like, civil society provides moral authority through authentic relationships and shared community at the individual level. Only such voluntary associations can provide authentic relationships, empowered participation, and a sense of true belonging.

Because civil society is also spontaneous. No one "sets it up." There is no central planning of happiness. It is voluntary. And through equal opportunity to pursue happiness, there emerges a self-ordering network of relationships and associations. As people pursue their own diverse goals and purposes, they plug into the network and find true inclusion.

CONCLUSION

Liberty Equality Fraternity

As we watch statues of historical figures come down and statues of criminals go up (they are the new heroes). As we watch black businesses burn to the ground and black police officers targeted in their own communities. As we cry "foul" each time we recognize injustice and that injustice goes unanswered, we should not only recognize the failure of CRT to produce any positive change, but observers should start to understand that it creates the problems it claims it seeks to solve.

Their thesis is false, this idea of oppression by the current system. The constitution and federalism ensures freedom, ensures choices (about where to live, what laws to abide by), and promotes civil liberties and natural rights, including equality. The very system CT advocates seek to overturn also serves as the framework within which we have overcome so much oppression in the past. Are we perfect? No, but the system in place has allowed for the greatest progress on the planet toward overcoming oppression, and thus eliminating it makes no sense.

There are rank and file members of Black Lives Matter whose hearts are in the right place. There are people who truly believe they were born in the wrong body. There are evil men and righteous women fighting the fight, but those people do not understand they are being used to advance an agenda that will not empower them as individuals, nor even as part of their defined "group," but will instead empower someone else, some other all-powerful entity, just like Communism (Marxism) did.

The citizens of the Soviet Union were not better off after the capitalists were overthrown and private property was abolished. A new group of central planners took over and starved to death those they did not kill outright. Mao's Cultural Revolution likewise did not leave the Chinese people who believed in it better off.

There is a reason that leaders of feminist groups don't care about the women in Afghanistan losing their rights – or their heads. There is a reason that leaders of LGBTQ groups don't care about gays being beaten and stoned or thrown off buildings in Iran. Or why cultural revolution leaders do not care about ethnic minorities or the freedom to pursue the arts in faraway lands. Because they aren't actually interested in liberties or culture or protecting the vulnerable. *Their goals have been accomplished* in Afghanistan with fascism back in control and freedoms eliminated.

They now have the space to accomplish the very same thing here. They are working toward that end in the hopes that they will be one of the elites with power, doing the oppressing with no care for their rank-and-file followers who will ultimately be more oppressed – and by their own leaders.[3]

Don't accept their premises, don't accept their statement of the thesis. Their goal, the strategic synthesis, cannot be introduced

---

[3] Remember how the BLM leadership was upset they were not included in the new Biden administration – and spent their money not to enrich or empower their followers, but to buy mansions?

unless those being manipulated take a side that will advance the predetermined agenda. So step outside the agenda.

Juneteenth serves a very important purpose and teaches a lesson those who believe they are oppressed by the system should heed. Juneteenth – 150 years late – is now codified as a federal holiday and very appropriately serves as a reminder to all Americans: You are free. Don't let anyone tell you or anyone you know that you are *not* equal, that you *don't* have rights, that you are *not* free.

Anyone who says you are not equal, that you don't have the same rights, that you are not free, can be likened to the deceitful enslavers in Texas. They are lying for their own benefit.

But also know that there are many who fall for this lie. They are free, but don't *feel* free, they are not living as though they are free, and thus they don't recognize their own freedom.

Everyone else: Don't stop telling them the good news: They are free too.

Remember the goal of Critical Theory: Destruction of the system, a reversal of power, to eliminate liberty and replace it with authoritarianism. Instead of allowing Juneteenth to serve the purposes of the fascist and racist ANTI-Thesis, allow it to serve its intended purpose, to celebrate freedom. Embrace the Jubilee!

Hard Truths

We have to change the narrative. No one is locked up in a garage somewhere. Yet some people *are* in garages and *don't know* the door is not locked. Those of us who see this have a responsibility to open the door to the garage and tell the self-imprisoned person they are free. We cannot drag them out of the garage against their will, but maybe after we stop by every day for a while, they will see they can open the door themselves and step outside. And if someone is there with a map and directions and helps them look for a bicycle or wants to share their car, they can get going on their way rather quickly.

Many challenge this idea of American equality and its connection to freedom. They want to know how to account for the *inequality* found in America even though there should be freedom. They cannot separate the two concepts and believe equality should be inextricably linked to freedom. This creates a crisis of conscience for them. How can this be a free society when there are still those living in poverty? What should our responsibility be toward those who are seeking Miami but were born in Alaska?

The truth is when we have freedom, we have the freedom to do good, to give to the poor, to build houses, to employ those who need a job, to train those who need it, to help people prepare for interviews, write recommendation letters, start a foundation, etc. We can use our resources for good. The problem comes from the fact that on our own we don't have enough resources to do *as much good* as we would like to do!

It is thus important to understand the working definition of equality before evaluating which concept should have priority: Freedom or equality? Is equality being treated with the same dignity? Is equality everyone having the same freedom to pursue our own happiness? Is equality when everyone, even our leaders, are subject to the same laws? If we see equality in an economic sense, then there can never be equality. There will always be at least two classes of people. Always. Americans often like to focus on socio-economic parity because it has been framed as the goal we should all be striving for. But what if the only way to achieve socio-economic parity is to ensure all people were equally poor? Would that solve the problem? Is that actually what we want?

Because the reality we've seen play out throughout all of history is that after a power reversal, we would still have two classes of people: The governing class, the elite, and then the rest of us.

So how do we account for the inequality in America even though we do have freedom? **We have inequality** *because* **we have freedom.** But that freedom allows us to do good. To treat people with equal dignity and all the rest. Yes, that freedom is also the freedom to do evil, to mistreat people. But that is why Americans historically see equality as equality of opportunity and equality under the law. And this is evident because when people *are* mistreated, everyone innately wants justice. And when people are *not* afforded equal opportunity, the same applies. We recognize injustice. We recognize mistreatment. We recognize evil. At least for the moment.

I fear that the more emphasis we put on socio-economic equality instead of equal dignity, equal opportunity, and equality under the law, the harder it will become to recognize when something goes awry in the land of the free and the easier it will become to look to some other entity to provide for our happiness after defining for us what our happiness should be.

We cannot guarantee the equal outcomes the concept of "fairness and justice" rely upon, even if that equal outcome is something as vague as "happiness." And we should not want to. We should all want to pursue our own happiness! And honestly, we should not want to tell *other* people what will make them happy and what *they* should do. Unless, perhaps, they ask our opinion. (But maybe not even then.) Do you like it when someone else believes they know better than you what you should do, what you actually want to do, what will make you ultimately happy?

And that is why civil society is so important. It is through voluntary association that people acquire the skills and habits necessary for self-governance. Things like cooperation, collaboration, and deliberation. Empowered participation in organizations of like-minded people of common vision fosters trust among individuals. The habit of voluntarily joining with others to achieve goals promotes self-reliance and self-initiative, which are indispensable to the idea of self-governance. And as people learn to achieve their goals (pursue their own happiness) without looking to government, not only does this increase their freedom, it enhances human dignity.

All people are born as unique human beings with very different qualities, talents, personalities, characteristics, and ambitions. We all have a place in this earth, and we all bring something different to the table. And we come together in diverse and inclusive spaces within the network of voluntary associations we call civil society.

Not only that, but the habits fostered in civil society teach people how to govern themselves, and that is what is necessary to preserve the limited constitutional government that was supposed to protect our natural rights, the natural rights recognized and supposedly protected by the system we put in place, the system proponents of Critical Theory wish to overthrow, abolish.

American Race

RACE

Race is a socially constructed system of categorizing humans largely based on observable physical features (phenotypes), such as skin color, and on ancestry. There is no scientific basis for or discernible distinction between racial categories.

The ideology of race has become embedded in our identities, institutions and culture and is used as a basis for discrimination and domination. It can even be difficult for those in support of racial justice to start sincere, authentic conversations about race.

The real question is why the American narrative on race has been framed the way it has. There truly is no scientific basis for the concept at all. We are all one human family, one "race" of humans. If race is a social construct, then why does the prevailing narrative serve to reinforce the concept they say they are seeking to educate out of us? They never miss an opportunity to throw out the term, link it to domination and oppression and inflame the passions to the point they overtake reason. What is the actual and ultimate goal or agenda of the proponents of Critical Theory? Of equity over equality? Of insisting racism isn't personal, but systemic and systematic? Who benefits? Who is empowered?

All I know is that it is not "the rest of us." I want to implore as many people as are willing to step outside of the false dialectic. Whatever the ultimate goal of all this division is, don't let it win. Build trust. Connect with your community. Develop authentic relationships. Encourage one another. Help one another. Respect one another. Use your gifts to complement theirs. But don't let them take the foundational unifying principle of this country away from us. Defend our natural rights. Defend your freedom. And then, passionately pursue your happiness.

EPILOGUE

It is about black and white. Just not in the way everyone thinks it is. Some people may frame it as right versus wrong, good versus evil, but then we fall into the trap that was laid for us. Saying that people can only belong to one group (good or bad, oppressed or oppressor) based upon a single idea or behavior is another premise that nullifies the argument of those arguing it. Rejecting the idea of the binary when it comes to gender and sex. Rejecting the idea of the binary when it comes to morality. Rejecting the idea of the binary when it comes to truth – yet demanding and working from an a priori position that there are only two options! This leads to the logic principle of non-contradiction which in the end nullifies the theory. If anything, the conclusion is that those arguing the truth of the theory are also arguing the falsehood of the theory.

People are not simply black or white. Each individual is way too complex to box into a single "side," regardless of what they believe. Those who fall for the lie that they themselves are that simple and allow themselves to be categorized by others instead of their unique personal characteristics enslave themselves and have voluntarily given up their natural right to pursue their own happiness. The good news is they can just as easily voluntarily give up their de facto enslavement because they are free to do so, because they are free.

They just have to recognize their freedom, their ability to choose for themselves what will make them happy.

This *should* be about black and white, but we are labeling a myriad of grays in between as either black or white. From a misunderstanding of how racial division and critical theory in general are being exploited, we are allowing a country once synonymous with freedom to be transformed, not into a utopia, but into a society intent on running on fear.

In the free world, the competition of ideas and of parties flourishes, and allegiances are often based on a single common principle or purpose that struggles against a competing point of view.

> Though generally healthy for a society, this competition can be quite dangerous if we lose sight of the fact that there is a far greater divide between the world of freedom and the world of fear than there is between the competing factions within a free society. If we fail to recognize this, we lose moral clarity. The legitimate differences among us, the shades of gray in a free society, will be wrongly perceived as black and white. Then, the real black-and-white line that divides free societies from fear societies, the real line that divides good from evil, will no longer be distinguishable.[…]A lack of moral clarity is why people living in free societies can come to see their fellow citizens as their enemies and foreign dictators as their friends. (Sharansky, 2006, xvii-xviii)

Do we want to belong to a group that resides in the gray and let that group define us as black or white? Or do we want to be a uniquely human individual with deeply personal aspirations and dreams, able to face personal challenges head on and either celebrate our successes or fail forward? Do we want to hand over our thinking and future to those who know better than we do what will make us happy? Or do we want to overcome limited expectations and forge our own destiny? Do we want to be enslaved to our emotions or free to pursue our happiness? Do we want to live in fear – or in freedom?

I am not writing this missive for approval from the masses, or even for approval from a few, or even approval from one. I am writing it in hopes that it will evoke an awakening in one, just one, person. And I am writing it:

For Walid Phares – A Lebanese American and the person whose thinking makes the most sense to me and who trusts me with knowing exactly what he is thinking himself.

For Yaneth Grajales – A Columbian who entered the United States illegally as a child (now a citizen) and who is the one person who always seems to know what I am thinking. More than any other person, she seems to "get" me.

For Denise Grant – My Antiguan friend (a legal alien, but not a citizen), together we are "Ebony and Ivory," making the music of life together. With no one else on this planet have I laughed so hard and enjoyed silent togetherness so much. She keeps me honest.

For Alan Eldridge – Full of ideas and passion and trust in me I never deserved. He is my constant reminder that we are all part of the same family and no matter where we started out or what circumstances shaped us after, we operate and celebrate and suffer together as one. (1 Corinthians 12:12-27)

For Emmanuel McNeely – A former student who gets it and does it. He goes to as many garages as possible and keeps opening the doors for those inside – and (sometimes even when they are still sitting in the garage) he encourages them by preparing them for the journey ahead, giving them a map, pointing the way, and connecting them to resources. He is still on his way toward happiness, and he is trying to take as many people with him as possible. A true inspiration.

None of the people above have fallen for the false premises of the false dialectic and never will. They are not ruled by their passions. They refuse to be manipulated into increased division and fear. These are people with an understanding of personal agency who have pushed past passion and rhetoric and who are thus truly empowered. America needs more people like them who are ready and willing to tell their stories, expand their sphere of influence, and demonstrate that true happiness is found in the pursuit of it. This is how we heal the divide, through true understanding and authentic relationships, not through promises made by politicians who have no intention of keeping them nor by mandating training programs that simply serve to reinforce ideas to keep us divided.

Each person is also much more complex as an individual than they are supposed to be when belonging to a group. The more people in any group automatically makes the social dynamics exponentially *more* complex, yet by assigning individuals to groups, those doing the assigning are attempting to simplify the social dynamics and "better understand" what the group needs to live a full and healthy life. How does this make sense? Each person has individual needs as well as individual hopes, dreams, desires, talents, gifts, ambitions, and passions. There cannot be a single way to look at every individual, assign them to some arbitrary group and thereby understand what will make that individual happy, yet that is the only way an immense and all-knowing power can even attempt to approach providing the resources necessary for a full and healthy life. To bring about equity, diversity must be sacrificed in thought and deed – and freedom must also be sacrificed on that same altar.

I also wrote this in memory of the diversity found in neighborhood of my childhood: The African American Seventh Day Adventists next door to us on Audubon Parkway, the Native Americans next door on the other side, and beside them, the Vietnamese family who did not speak any English – as well as the Arab Muslims across the street and the Arab Christians down the street.

We were all so different from one another, yet we all belonged to and found connections within the same community.

I wrote this in memory of the "multi-cultural" (Korean, Ghanan, Arab, African American, Chinese, Christian, Muslim, Jewish and Hindu) friendships of my childhood and college years that seemed so easy because no one told us they weren't supposed to be.

I wrote this to celebrate the South Florida congregations I served in, consisting of Jamaicans, Haitians, Puerto Ricans, Brazilians, Cubans, Indians, Koreans, Chinese, Iranians, Columbians, African Americans, and just, well, Americans.

And in honor of my entire crazy family, from Phuong to Julius and all the cousins in between.

All of you and so many others create the colorful tableau upon which I see not only the majestic possibilities of what this country could be, but what it once was for me and how that majesty pales in comparison to the splendor and majesty that is to come.

There was a time when we did not label people or set them apart due to some immutable characteristic. I still remember it. Maybe that is what we call "childhood" today. Oh that we could all become children again. For the Kingdom of Heaven belongs to such as these.

REFERENCES

Karl Marx. The German Ideology. 1845.

McGuire, Angus (Artist). Image Illustrating Equality VS Equity: Interaction Institute for Social Change. Credit to: interaction-institute.org & madewithangus.com

Hegel, G. W. F. (1956). *The Philosophy of History*. New York: Dover Publications, Inc. (Republication of final translation by J. Sibree, The Colonial Press: 1899).

Nix, Elizabeth. (2015, June 19). What is Juneteenth? Juneteenth Commemorates an Effective End to Slavery in the United States. (Updated 2022, June 22). Retrieved from https://www.history.com/news/what-is-juneteenth

Annie E. Casey Foundation. (2020, August 24). Equity vs. Equality and Other Racial Justice Definitions. Retrieved from: https://www.aecf.org/blog/racial-justice-definitions (Updated 2021, April 14).

Sharansky, N. (2006). Preface (pp. ix – xxvi). *The case for democracy: The power of freedom to overcome tyranny and terror.* New York: Public Affairs.

AUTHOR'S NOTE

I was encouraged by all participants to write a book based upon my May 2022 *Freedom Academy with Dorothy* webinar entitled "The Unraveling," which spoke to the destruction of the fabric of American society. In the midst of turning eight pages of notes into 200 pages of text, I found myself off the intended path and quite a distance down a rabbit trail, discussing critical theory, so I took a quick break from *The Unraveling* and spent six days in July 2022 writing this quick essay. It is virtually unchanged from the July 2022 version, but I could not in good conscience release this short essay before the larger work from which it was birthed. Both works complement one another – and while there may be two or three shared sentences (or ideas) between the two, this subject was too hefty to simply include as a chapter within the larger work—and too independent from the overarching theme of *The Unravelling* to easily incorporate it within. I just could not get it to "fit" (not to mention, the style of writing differs between the two). I do, however, hope readers will engage both works in concert with one another. As each makes the other make more sense.